Patty's Parables
Earthly Stories
with Heavenly
Meanings

By
Patty L. Graham

Patty L. Graham

ISBN: 1505698421
ISBN-13: 978-1505698428

TABLE OF CONTENTS

TABLE OF CONTENTS CONT.

INTRODUCTION

The Creator of the Universe spoke into existence everything on earth, including human beings. He still desires to reveal answers to life's questions and mysteries to us. The author hopes that these daily devotionals will inspire, provoke and encourage every reader to tune in to the voice of their creator and draw closer to the One who created them. Let each story reveal how our Creator desires to communicate with everyone daily!

1

The Helper Is Here

One morning I heard the voice of the Lord say "I am the Helper; I AM here to help you. I am answering the prayer "Help Me." At that time I wasn't sure what God meant so I got up and went out back with my dog. My attention was drawn to a section in my backyard where weeds and thorns had taken over an area that is now the rock garden. I was compelled to root them out. I am not usually compelled to dig out weeds. As a child, I thought it cruel and unusual child labor that I had to pull weeds. I would rather do almost anything else! My husband, Bill, and I had discussed a rock garden. We thought there had been one in this area before, but at this time it was a mess. I grabbed a hoe and a rake and began pounding the ground. Each time I pulled out a weed or thorn structure I unearthed beautiful stones that had been buried nderneath. "It's time for the stones to cry out for My presence!" I was impressed by God. I suddenly had an unusual desire and strength to get these weeds out. Thorns stuck through my gloves. Prongs bent on my rake and the head of the hoe flew off. Holy Spirit said, "Water it!" I sprayed a hard stream over it, dirt flew off and rocks moved and glistened!" "Now wash the rocks with the water of the Word." I declared that "living stones would be unearthed and cry out until the presence of God is established in our territory." I heard Him say "Keep

2

plowing until it is completed. It's time for the Bride to work the garden for the Bridegroom. Restore what the Creator started until my presence is in the earth." My husband is a geologist. God said, "Take a picture and tell him you made him a rock garden. Then present it to the Lord as a work from the Bride to the Bridegroom." In the past, I would never do anything like this without Bill. This is a picture of what God is doing in the earth today. The Living Stone and a Chosen People. As we come to Him, the Living Stone, rejected by humans but chosen by God and precious to Him, you also, like living stones, are being built into a spiritual house to be a holy priesthood, offering spiritual sacrifices acceptable to God through Jesus Christ. For in scripture it says: *"See I lay a stone in Zion, a chosen and precious cornerstone, and the one who trusts in Him will never be put to shame."* 1 Peter 2:6

PRAYER FOR THE DAY: Father, show me where the weeds and thorns have covered up my identity and purpose. Holy Spirit, plow up the beauty within me and reveal your purposes. Restore in me the joy of my salvation today! I ask for Your Presence to invade every area of my life!

ACTIVATION: Let Holy Spirit reveal to you what might be hindering your purpose and identity. Ask Holy Spirit to show you what changes to make to uncover the identity He is forming in you.

2

Arise In God's Authority

One morning I experienced what I call a
waking vision. I had been dreaming
and awoke with a vivid ending to the
dream, hearing a song. The dream was
straight out of the movie "Lord of the
Rings." The scene was where those
who had covenanted to help Frodo take
the ring to its destination to be
destroyed were ascending a
mountainous pass in a snow storm.
They had unified for a mission to 'save
the world'. One of the team yelled,
"There's a foul sound in the air." Their
enemy was speaking curses against
them into the atmosphere. The leader
of the group, Gandalf, began to counter
the curses, but before it was thwarted

a dangerous avalanche broke loose from the curses and buried the party under snow. Driven to the more dangerous route now, they shifted to move through the mountain where their warfare increased. Entering the mountain required the right declaration. Throughout the dangerous trek, it was SOUND that caused their momentum. Warring their way through, they came to a point where a dreaded ancient demon awakened to confront them. The leader instructed the others to quickly escape across the deadly collapsing bridge. The weapons they had used in the past battles would not work in this one. Surrounded by attacking enemies and with ultimate evil pursuing, the bridge to their safety crumbles as they cross. The ancient evil rises as the last one passes. The leader is now facing off the enemy. Slamming his rod of authority to the ground, he decrees "YOU SHALL NOT PASS!!" Lightning and thunder roar from his rod of authority, forcefully knocking the enemy back. The team escapes. In my waking vision, I am the leader that has to face off the enemy with a rod of authority and a declaration. I woke up doing so while hearing a song by Glory of Zion International titled "The Swords Will Contend." I hear them calling me, The Spirit and the Bride to Be, Come everyone to drink All who are thirsty, Against the storm, Against the tide, Against all odds I will rise, I will rise, I will rise.

Luke 10:19

[19] I have given you authority to trample on snakes and scorpions and to overcome all the power of the enemy; nothing will harm you.

PRAYER FOR THE DAY: Thank You Lord that You know what I will deal with today and what I need for this day. I receive all power and authority to push back the enemy and receive the victory you bought for me on the cross. Fill me with your victorious Spirit today!

ACTIVATION: Ask Holy Spirit to show you where you need victory today and then ask Holy Spirit to give you victory over something. Note where that victory is.

3

Pride Goes Before a Fall

I love thunder storms. They remind me of God's power and love for us. One morning I awoke to the sound of thunder and heard the song "How Great Thou Art." I don't actually know the lyrics to this song so I looked them up. I discovered there were verses written that we don't sing that are very appropriate for the United States as a nation right now. We tend to be a proud nation. We pride ourselves on our ability to achieve, but it wasn't our ability that made this nation what it is. God is calling us all to humility. God is the one who gives us everything. We must honor Him and His ways to stay a "blessed nation." Power comes only from the Lord. Humility and love are what God requires for us to see His power. God desires us to stand up for truth, in humility. Jesus showed us how to accomplish this by walking in truth and compassion in the midst of constant criticism and persecution. He moved in power because He walked in love.

Below are the lyrics to "How Great Thou Art". I pray that it speaks to your spirit and causes you to remember where true freedom comes from. There are two verses here that are generally omitted from hymnals in the U.S.A. O when I see ungrateful man defiling this bounteous earth, God's gifts so good and great: In foolish pride, God's holy Name reviling, and yet, in grace, His wrath and judgment wait. When burdens press, and seem beyond

endurance, bowed down with grief, to
Him I lift my face; and then in love He
brings me sweet assurance: 'My Child!
For thee sufficient is my grace. O Lord
my God, When I in awesome wonder,
consider all the works Thy hand hath
made, I see the stars, I hear the
mighty thunder, Thy power throughout
the universe displayed; When through
the woods, and forest glades I wander,
I hear the birds sing sweetly in the
trees. When I look down from lofty
mountain grandeur, and hear the brook
and feel the gentle breeze; Then sings
my soul, My Savior God to Thee, How
great thou art! Then sings my soul, My
Savior God, to Thee, How great Thou
art! How Great Thou Art! When Christ
shall come, with shouts of acclamation,
and take me home, what joy shall fill my

heart! Then I shall bow in humble
adoration and there proclaim, "My God,
How Great Thou Art!"
*2 Chronicles 7:14 ¹⁴ if my people, who
are called by my name, will humble
themselves and pray and seek my face
and turn from their wicked ways, then I
will hear from heaven, and I will forgive
their sin and will heal their land.*

PRAYER: Lord, as I humble myself
today and seek Your face, remind me of
Your great love for me and my nation,
wherever I may live. Remind me how I
got to this time and place and how You
desire me to move into my destiny
today.

ACTIVATION: Look for the ways the Lord has blessed you today. Thank Him for all that He has done. Write how He reveals you are blessed.

4

Agree With God

Have you ever thought about how
incredible it is that the God of the
Universe loves you and wants to talk to
you? God is really big and He does big
miraculous things, like opening up the
Red Sea for the Israelites to pass
through, and Jesus healing blind and
paralyzed people and even raising the
dead. The fact that He wants to be
intimately involved in our daily lives
amazes me even more. The Creator of
the Universe wants to talk to us about
our every day lives. He wants to
fellowship with us even more than we
do! That's incredible! One day I was
cleaning my dining room and I noticed
some money under the table. When I

picked it up it was a two dollar bill.
Unusual, I thought. I heard the Lord
say "If you will agree with me, I will
multiply your supply." Of course I
thought that was great and agreed! AS
I continued to dust the knick knacks on
my fireplace mantle, the Lord impressed
me to rearrange things. A friend had
given me a ceramic piece that looks like
the legs and ruby slippers of
the wicked witch of the west, from the
Wizard of Oz movie. The shoes are the
ones Dorothy's house landed on and
that she wore to click her heals to go
home. Dorothy had to agree to do
some very interesting actions to get
home in that movie. She agreed to go
to the wizard to get strategy to get
home, then to get the witches broom,
then she had to believe if she clicked

her heals together she'd go home. I realize it's a movie, but the metaphor is interesting. We must agree with God that He will give us strategies to get where we need to be and then obey even when it doesn't make sense to us. The Bible is full of stories like this. Faith and action go hand in hand. Even prophetic actions. So God impressed me to put the shoes under the small treasure chest on my fireplace mantle so that it looks like the scene from the movie with the house on the legs with the shoes sticking out. Instead of a house, it was a treasure chest for my supply that He said He would multiply. Now I understood the picture. Then I heard Him say, "Declare ding dong with witch is dead, and she can no longer steal my

inheritance." What can it hurt?? As I did, I was impressed with the verse *in Isaiah 45:3, I will give you hidden treasures, riches stored in secret places, so that you may know that I am the Lord, the God of Israel, who summons you by name.*
Matthew 18:19 "Again, truly I tell you that if two of you on earth agree about anything they ask for, it will be done for them by my Father in heaven.

PRAYER: Lord, help me today to hear and obey what You are saying to me. Teach me to take a risk and apply my faith to see you move in a new way in my life. Thank you that you desire to be involved in every aspect of my life.

ACTIVATION: Ask God to show you someone to bless today by giving them an encouraging call, a gift or card.

5

It's Transformation Time

Transformation is defined as: thorough
or dramatic change in form or
appearance. Some synonyms: change,
alteration, mutation, conversion,
metamorphosis, transfiguration,
transmutation, and change. We are all
given every opportunity to cooperate
with Holy Spirit to become all we were
put on the earth to be. Most of the time
this involves some 'irritations' to our
flesh and some uncomfortable
cocooning to achieve God's desired
outcome. How many times have you
had to deal with some irritating
situations and people, only to realize
God was working on your character? I
know I have. Joseph went through it,

Daniel went through it, Esther and
more. The biblical story of Jacob comes
to mind. Jacob's older twin brother was
totally opposite of Jacob. Esau was
firstborn and was supposed to get the
birthright blessing, but Jacob and his
mother tricked Esau and Isaac, their
father, into giving it to Jacob. This
deception sets Esau on edge and causes
Jacob to flee for his life. Jacob enters
into a fourteen year transformation time
of labor and reaping the rewards of this
action. Jacob encounters God coming
and going into this process of
transformation where God reveals his
true identity and changes him from
deceiver to promised one. Heaven
opens over Jacob as he rests on his way
to the place of "irritation and
transformation." When Jacob leaves

to return to his home and face his fear
of confrontation with his brother, he
wrestles with the angel of the Lord over
his new identity and the blessings.

Genesis 32:24-29

*So Jacob was left alone, and a man
wrestled with him till daybreak. When
the man saw that he could not
overpower him, he touched the socket
of Jacob's hip so that his hip was
wrenched as he wrestled with the man.
Then the man said, "Let me go, for it is
daybreak." But Jacob replied, "I will not
let you go unless you bless me."
The man asked him, "What is your
name?" "Jacob," he answered.
Then the man said, "Your name will no
longer be Jacob, but Israel, because you
have struggled with God and with
humans and have overcome."*

Jacob said, "Please tell me your name."
But he replied, "Why do you ask my
name?" Then he blessed him there.
Jacob, limping, faces his fear, resolving
the conflict with his brother.
Opportunities to allow the irritations of
life can make us bitter or better. God
will use all things to work together for
our good if we allow Him to 'transform'
us and renew our minds. Many people
in the Bible received new names which
reflected their transformed identities.
These new names are God's way of
revealing His divine plan and to assure
them that God's plan could be fulfilled.
Romans 12:2
Do not conform to the pattern of this
world, but be **transformed** *by the*
renewing of your mind. Then you will be
able to test and approve what God's will

is—his good, pleasing and
perfect will.

PRAYER: Thank You Lord that You
desire to transform me into a new
creation that reveals Your nature and
purpose in the earth. Help me through
each irritating situation to see how you
are transforming me into Your image.

ACTIVATION: Ask Holy Spirit to show
you what 'irritations' He has brought
into your life to help develop your new
identity. Then ask Him to
show you how to walk through this test
to get to the next place He has for you.

6

Driven By Communication

Communications can be defined as: the
activity of communicating; the activity of
conveying information; something that
is communicated by or to or between
people or groups; a connection allowing
access between persons or places; ex.
"how many lines of communication can
there be among four people?"
Communication is a process of
transferring information from one entity
to another. Communication processes
are sign mediated interactions between
at least two agents which share a
repertoire of signs and semiotic rules.
We are a communication driven society.
We thrive on connections and how we
can relate. I recently saw a report that

said many Americans do not truly 'relate to one another' in a human connection type fashion; we have become electronic addicts. We Tweet, Facebook, text, email, and Skype, but can we turn it all off and actually relate to someone? I am grateful for all of these communication devises. They have made a way for us to stay in contact. I rarely used Skype before my son moved to Florida, but I certainly learned to use it then. I wanted to be able to connect with him. A few years ago a communications company used a slogan "reach out and touch someone" to encourage consumers to use their company to make phone calls. We were not really 'touching' people in the tactile sense, but connecting through communications. I used to be a personal assistant where I would do tasks and many times go to ten or more destinations such as stores, post office, and cleaners. I would stay in touch with my boss by phone or text. One day, my phone went blank. I could not connect. I could not text, call, email, or communicate any way. I did not know what to do. I tried calling everyone, texting, emailing, but could not reach anyone any of those ways. I actually had a brief moment of anxiety wondering what to do. I had to keep going and pray. God really wants to connect with His children. The Lord revealed to me that He is constantly trying to contact us to communicate information, but we are not always connected or in tune to His frequency. He is sending signals and looking for those who can help us learn to connect with Him. Many people's lives would be totally changed by hearing that God really wants to connect with them. We can be the communication device for others as we choose to tune in and share what He is saying.

John 10:16

*I have other sheep, which are not **of** this fold; I must bring **them** also, and **they** will hear My **voice**; and **they** will become one flock with one **shepherd**.*

PRAYER: Father, help me connect with You today to hear your voice and come into a deeper relationship with You. Help me to share how You want to speak to all Your children because you love them.

ACTIVATION: Ask God to show you how to communicate a message from Him with someone today. Note how this encourages and blesses others.

7

God's Treasure

Our ministry team loves to do new things. We heard about "Treasure Hunts" and were lead to read Kevin Dedmon's book The Ultimate Treasure Hunt. What is the most important treasure in the earth? Gold, precious jewels or silver? No, it's human beings. God loves us so much that He wants to have a personal relationship with each and every person. If we are not on His frequency to communicate with Him, we cannot hear Him or sense Him or relate to Him. That is unless you know Jesus Christ. Jesus said that His sheep hear His voice. He connects us to the Father through His Spirit so we can hear, see, feel, the messages Father is sending us.

Jesus met daily with God and then did what He saw His Father doing. He told us to do the same thing and even greater things. So I decided to try this treasure hunt idea. I asked the Lord to give me 'clues' every day to find His treasures and connect them to Him. The clues came faster than I could write along with the divine encounters. One clue was a pink shirt with a bumble bee. That sounds strange, but God told me what to tell the person and to pray with them. I went to a Zumbathon and turned around to see a lady wearing a pink shirt with a bumblebee. WOW! I could not have missed that if I tried. God had an encouraging message for me to give to her that really helped her that day. Before I knew it I was getting clues from God everyday and seeing

people's lives changed everywhere. God
kept telling me about wrists. I prayed
for more people with wrist problems,
and saw them healed, than ever before.
He told me to pray for the wrists of the
body of Christ. Without my wrists,
typing would be pretty difficult. I would
be limited in many ways. God is ready
to reveal His love to His treasures. They
are just waiting to be discovered and
connected to him. We can be the ones
that touch them with the love of God
and the connection to God they need.
God wants to heal, bless, encourage
and be reconciled to His children.
Without that connection many are like I
was without my phone. I was going
about my daily activities unable to
access the person I needed to get my
instructions, direction and clarity from.

Ananias was a man of prayer. One day
God shifted Ananias to act on what He
showed Him. Acts 9 shows how
important this can be: *Acts 9:11-15*
*¹¹ The Lord told him, "Go to the house
of Judas on Straight Street and ask for a
man from Tarsus named Saul, for he is
praying. ¹² In a vision he has seen a
man named Ananias come and place his
hands on him to restore his sight."*
*¹³ "Lord," Ananias answered, "I have
heard many reports about this man and
all the harm he has done to your holy
people in Jerusalem. ¹⁴ And he has come
here with authority from the chief
priests to arrest all who call on your
name." ¹⁵ But the Lord said to Ananias,
"Go! This man is my chosen instrument
to proclaim my name to the Gentiles
and their kings and to the people of*

Israel.

PRAYER: Lord, help me to hear your voice and act on Your promptings today. Thank You for desiring to communicate with me and have a relationship with me.

ACTIVATION: Ask the Lord to give you 'clues' and for encouragement or to pray for healing for someone today. Look for the person and be ready to act on it like Ananias.

8

It's Time to Run

We used to live in a city neighborhood.
God made it very clear that He wanted
us to move into a rural area with some
land. He also wanted us to get rid of
our mortgage debt. His strategy was to
buy more land and a house. I did not
understand how that could even work,
but I agreed to obey and began
searching. We found a place that
needed to be transformed. It was a
mess but this was evidently where God
wanted us. I asked God, if this was the
place that He wanted us to buy and
move to, that He would give me a dog.
Not just any dog. I wanted a black and
white Australian Shepherd with blue
eyes that was trained and ready to be

on this land. The day after we decided to buy this place some friends I had not seen in twenty-six years put a picture of Booger, my dog now, on Facebook asking if anyone wanted him. I called them and set up a time to meet the dog to see if this was a fit. When we met it was evident to all of us that this was my dog. The house and land then went into auction. We bought the house. God revealed His strategy to reduce debt and enlarged our territory. The first two weeks at the new house, we had to keep Booger on a leash because he runs very fast and could jump the fences, which needed to be fixed. He could easily get out of his boundaries, which could be dangerous for him. The day we finished fixing the fence we let him off the leash. The land is landscaped and tiered. He flew off each tier running like the wind completely around his borders. He returned to us smiling and panting. He was ready to handle an enlarged boundary. Booger mostly answers when we call, unless distracted by squirrels, cows, deer or a lizard. The other day when my husband was up on a ladder putting light bulbs on the motion detectors, Booger found a place on the fence that he could jump over. He was very excited about a young man who was jogging down the road, so he got out to run with him. We were able to get him to answer to our call, because outside of our boundaries is danger in the woods. God is extending our boundaries and giving us new freedom to hear and obey Him in an enlarged territory. It is up to us to

obey when He calls so that we reap all
the benefits of the blessings that He has
for us. Outside of our boundaries can
be dangerous. If we fall into old
patterns of behavior God has to begin
training us again. Ask God to help you
to hear and obey Him quickly, so that
you can reap the benefits of an enlarged
territory.

1 Chronicles 4:10

*Jabez cried out to the God of Israel,
"Oh, that you would bless me and
enlarge my territory! Let your hand be
with me, and keep me from harm so
that I will be free from pain." And God
granted his request.*

PRAYER: Lord, help me to hear and obey You today. Bless me and enlarge my territories and boundaries and show me how to be a blessing in this new place.

ACTIVATION: Ask the Lord to show you what He would have you do today that would enlarge your boundaries, spiritually, or naturally.

9

What Do You See?

Distractions are everywhere. When we are trying to pray, seek God, or see what He's saying, it seems like we can see dirt that we didn't see before. Sometimes everything that we need to accomplish flashes through our minds, our phones ring or ding with messages that just can't seem to wait.

Throughout the Bible, God asked people what they saw. God gives us insight and spiritual vision to 'see' or 'perceive' what He is conveying to us. The story of Zaccheus in the New Testament is an interesting picture of how we can position ourselves to 'see' Jesus. When he did this, Zaccheus had an encounter that changed his life as well as others that his life impacted.

Luke 19:1-10 Jesus entered Jericho and was passing through. ² A man was there by the name of Zacchaeus; he was a chief tax collector and was wealthy. ³ He wanted to see who Jesus was, but because he was short he could not see over the crowd. ⁴ So he ran ahead and climbed a sycamore-fig tree to see him, since Jesus was coming that way.
⁵ When Jesus reached the spot, he looked up and said to him, "Zacchaeus, come down immediately. I must stay at your house today." ⁶ So he came down at once and welcomed him gladly. ⁷ All the people saw this and began to mutter, "He has gone to be the guest of a sinner." ⁸ But Zacchaeus stood up and said to the Lord, "Look, Lord! Here and now I give half of my possessions to the

poor, and if I have cheated anybody out of anything, I will pay back four times the amount." [9] *Jesus said to him, "Today salvation has come to this house, because this man, too, is a son of Abraham.* [10] *For the Son of Man came to seek and to save the lost."*

Zaccheus was so divinely impacted by seeing Jesus that he repented, totally changing the direction of his life. He was ready to act on the revelation that Jesus was the Messiah which he received when he encountered the Lord. Matthew Henry's concise commentary says it like this: Those who sincerely desire a sight of Christ, like Zaccheus, will break through opposition, and take pains to see him. Christ invited himself to Zaccheus' house. Wherever Christ

comes He opens the heart, and inclines
it to receive him. He that has a mind to
know Christ shall be known of him.
Those, whom Christ calls, must humble
themselves and come down. We may
well receive him joyfully, who brings all
good with him. Zaccheus gave proofs
publicly that he had become a true
convert. He does not look to be
justified by his works, as the Pharisees,
but by his good works he will, through
the grace of God, show the sincerity of
his faith and repentance. Zaccheus is
declared to be a happy man, new he is
turned from sin to God. Now that he is
saved from his sins, from the guilt of
them, from the power of them, all the
benefits of salvation are his. Christ is
come to his house, and where Christ
comes he brings salvation with him. He

seeks those that sought him not and asked not for him.

PRAYER: Lord, position me today to see Jesus in a new way that brings me into the new place of revelation you have for me. Thank You for loving me so much that you sent Jesus to show me Your ways.

ACTIVATION: Ask the Lord to show you something new about Him that will shift you!

10

Look At the Fruit

I've had one root canal on my teeth. It
was rather enlightening for me, to say
the least. During a root canal, the
nerve and pulp are removed and the
inside of the tooth is cleaned and sealed
to prevent infection and abscesses. The
dentist gave me gas to relax me during
the procedure. When I left, I was still a
little in the twilight zone, feeling no
pain. The left side of my face was
totally numb and I couldn't move it. I
needed to go to the grocery store,
although I knew I looked pretty strange
and couldn't smile or talk well. I hurried
through the store, setting a lip gloss in
the top of the basket to buy. After
checking out, as I was walking out to

the car, I realized they did not charge me for the lip gloss. The lip gloss was still in the basket. I put the lip gloss in my purse and started driving down the street. The Lord said, "So, are you just going to steal the lip gloss?" I was very uncomfortable and argued with God that I looked and felt bad. He replied "I do not really care how you look or feel, you need to do the right thing and take that back and pay for it." Squirming, I complied. I really just wanted to drive up to the store and throw the gloss at the front door and yell, "I didn't mean to steal it!" So, with my melting face, in my zoned out state, I went in to the "self check". It did not work. Uggghhhh! I then went to the cashier with my receipt and tried to explain what happened, with a droop and a drool I am sure. She acted as though she really could not understand what I was saying and just replied "okay'. She flippantly checked me out. I then realized there was a "root" that God was working out of me. Wow. I really do not like to look or sound stupid and am a little self conscious. Well there you have it. My fear of what man thinks, was rotten and needed to be rooted out. It is time to allow the Lord to reveal what may be keeping us from producing fruit that He desires in our lives. Sometimes the rooting out hurts a little but it is well worth it. The process will bring good fruit that lasts.

PRAYER: Lord, shine your light on the roots in my life that are producing unhealthy fruit. Root out and cleanse what is not from you, so I can be fruitful for your Kingdom. In Jesus name, amen.

ACTIVATION: Ask the Lord to reveal anything that He wants to root out of your life and then cooperate with Holy Spirit to begin the process.

11

What Keys Do You Have?

I have a lot of keys. I have keys to my house, three cars, the building our ministry is housed in, ministry office and studio, the keys to mailboxes, filing cabinets, storage units, and more. I have to separate my keys and categorize them so I remember which keys unlock what door. Some of my keys look similar, which can be confusing. I bought a picture of a lion with keys, representing the Lion of Judah obtaining the keys to death and hell. Obviously, keys are important in the Kingdom of God. Keys represent authority and access. God has given us keys to the Kingdom. *Matthew 16:19*
¹⁹ I will give you the keys of the

*kingdom of heaven; whatever you bind
on earth will be bound in heaven, and
whatever you loose on earth will
beloosed in heaven."*

*"Revelation 1:18 I am the Living One; I
was dead, and now look, I am alive for
ever and ever! And I hold the keys of
death and Hades. Isaiah 22:22 I will
place on his shoulder the key to the
house of David; what he opens no one
can shut, and what he shuts no one can
open.*

Keys are given to us to open doors and
things where we have been *given
authority.* There is an anointing that
goes with this authority and God is
showing us it's time to understand our
anointing and how to use the keys that
He has given us. I cannot use the
wrong key to open my door or safe or

car, it must belong to me and be the correct key. I cannot take a key that looks like the correct key and expect it to work. I have tried it. When I use the correct key with the correct anointing doors open and I can move in the areas I was meant to move in. This is a spiritual principal that the Lord wants us to understand in this season. I cannot expect to use your keys to open my doors and vice versa. This past week I had at least two key experiences that got my attention. I was at the healing rooms early and had opened the doors and entered with no problems. I went outside to get something and I used the correct key to lock the door but it got stuck and would not move. I found the maintenance man and asked him to put oil on it to see if it would fix it. He did

and it   worked. I heard the Lord say
"You need a new anointing for this
season." Then when I came home, my
son was trying to open the back door to
take out the garbage and he begin
shaking the door because the lock was
stuck. I heard the Lord say "I'm going
shake out everything that doesn't move
with the new anointing for this new
door." Both doors were doors with
locks I had authority over, but it was
time to receive a NEW anointing to
move through them to achieve what
God wanted in a new season.

PRAYER: Lord I receive your new
anointing! Father I ask for the keys that
you have for me today! Show me when
and how to use them by your Spirit.

ACTIVATION: Ask God to show you specifically where He has given you authority and how He would have you use your keys.

12

Too Many Choices

I once heard a man from Africa speaking at a conference. I'll never forget when he said "Americans have too many choices. I went to eat at a restaurant and asked for toast. They listed the types of bread and I got confused and said, "I just want toast." How true that is. We are a blessed nation with great abundance. With all that freedom comes great responsibility. Remember that Jesus said "*...To whom much is given, much is required...*" Luke *12:48* . We have been given the ability and freedom to choose eternal life, or not, to choose abundant life, or not, to choose to do the right thing, or not, to believe God, or not. The list is huge.

With each choice we make, we either further the Kingdom of God, or not. Maybe not by the choice of bread you eat, but definitely by the choices you make in life. How you choose is important. Many nations do not have the same choices and liberties that the U.S.A. has. Many places do not truly have freedom of speech or choices that we have. If you try to express your faith in many places you could be persecuted severely, but we can still choose. We may be rejected for doing the right thing but we still have the right to do it. When we obey God He extends His grace and He is pleased with our faith. A few years ago the slogan "What would Jesus do?" was very popular. The phrase came from a book about a pastor who challenged his congregation

to ask that question before making
decisions to affect their choices. Maybe
it is time to take that challenge.
I believe this is something we need to
review every day, every minute of our
lives. Are we making choices based on
what we want or on God's will? I
watched a movie titled <u>Evan Almighty.</u>
It was about a man who was just
elected to Congress and decides to
move his family to a new beginning. He
has got a plan for his life and he is
working it. He is not necessarily a
religious man, however his wife and kids
pray and bring to his attention that he
has promised to "change the world" and
that he might need God's help. So he
decides to pray. After a number of
bizarre incidents, Evan realizes God is
answering his prayer, but not the way

he thought. Now Evan has to make a
choice to either do his will or God's will.
At this point, he tells God that this was
not his plan for life. God laughs and
asks "Your plan?" Like the Noah of the
Bible, Evan is persecuted, laughed at,
mocked, and threatened. But a flood
really does come, people are saved, and
realize that God really did speak to Evan
as He had spoken to Noah. It is a great
picture of how our obedience to God
truly affects everyone and everything
around us. It may not be the most
popular thing but, in the end, always
the best. It's amazing how God chooses
us then helps us do great things when
we choose His plan instead of ours.
Many of us keep telling God we want to
see His Kingdom come and His will
done. Maybe it is time for us to

cooperate with God. You may be one choice away from the greatest manifestation of God you could ever imagine.

Joshua 24:15 But if serving the LORD seems undesirable to you, then choose for yourselves this day whom you will serve, whether the gods your ancestors served beyond the Euphrates, or the gods of the Amorites, in whose land you are living. But as for me and my household, we will serve the LORD."

PRAYER: Thank You Lord for the ability to choose eternal life. Help me today to make choices that will glorify You and bring Your Kingdom into our atmosphere. Thank You for giving me what I need to accomplish the things You give me to do.

ACTIVATION: Ask the Lord to help you consciously base your choices on what Jesus would do today. Note how you make different decisions based on the awareness of your choices.

13

Your Season Can Change

One Spring my husband and I were
compelled to plant a vegetable garden.
Neither of us are gardeners. We did
what we knew to do, prepared the soil,
planted and watered. As the summer
brought some tomatoes, green beans,
peppers and squash, it also caused
some plants to die. Something very
interesting started happening when we
began to have a lot of rain. Some
plants sprang up and began to tangle
with others. The garden became a
jungle of mixed up squash, green beans
and tomatoes and we could not tell
where one started and another one
ended. We thought this would surely
kill everything, but to our surprise things

were flourishing. The latter summer rain produced more good fruit than the earlier summer. Dead limbs and plants wound around the live, fruit producing limbs, which made it difficult to see where the produce was. After a good rain, the Lord lead me around the garden and said "look at this angle." Then He led me to another angle. I began to discover some of the biggest, healthiest green beans I have ever seen. The Lord showed me where and how to separate the dead plants from the living so that I could see and reap the harvest. Matthew 13:24-29 came to mind. *24 Jesus told them another parable: "The kingdom of heaven is like a man who sowed good seed in his field. 25 But while everyone was sleeping, his enemy came and sowed weeds among the wheat, and went away. ²⁶ When the wheat sprouted and formed heads, then the weeds also appeared. ²⁷ "The owner's servants came to him and said, 'Sir, didn't you sow good seed in your field? Where then did the weeds come from?' ²⁸ "'An enemy did this,' he replied. "The servants asked him, 'Do you want us to go and pull them up?' ²⁹ "'No,' he answered, 'because while you are pulling the weeds, you may uproot the wheat with them.* The Lord wants us to be careful how we reap our harvest. Many times we think something is covered over in death but underneath He has been cultivating life. He is just asking us to look again for the good fruit. Wherever His seed is planted it will produce something good.

PRAYER: Father, today show me where to look for my harvest. Let me look again and see the harvest that is ready for me to reap for Your Kingdom.

ACTIVATION: Ask God to help you look beyond what you see with your natural eyes. Ask Him to show you your garden and how to get the harvest.

14

Dream Again

When I was young I loved music and dancing. I secretly had a dream to be a dancer. I only shared that dream a few times. I did teach colour guard for a while. I took dance classes in college and later continued at various times. At one point the Lord gave me a dream of myself leading many people in dance. It was very skilled, yet very spiritual. After that the Lord led me to take more dance classes and start a dance team. I've

been doing it ever since. It is time to dream again. If the enemy has stolen your dream, it is time to recover it. In the book of Genesis, Joseph dreamed and interpreted dreams. He dreamed

God's plan for his life. He was also able to communicate his dream revelation. His brothers understood what God wanted to do as well. Because they were jealous they sold Joseph into slavery. God used the whole situation to bring Joseph into his dream and destiny. Joseph chose to allow his circumstances to make him better instead of bitter. When the time was right, he was released from prison to the palace to rule as a governmental leader in Egypt and deliver all of Egypt and the surrounding territory, even his family, from a devastating famine.

Read the story in Genesis 37-46. It is worth reading and praying through your dreams, betrayals and loss of vision. God is faithful and still wants you to fulfil the dreams and destiny that He put in your heart. Many times discouragement tends to overtake us in the midst of moving into our dreams. God can take discouragement and build your faith to overcome and become

everything He created you to be. Like Joseph, you must choose to remember what God has shown you and believe that God is well able to get you to the place that He has shown you. God is looking for those, like Joseph, who will walk in love, forgiveness, faith and destiny. Joseph was given a plan to save his family and a nation during a time of economic need. When it was time for Joseph's dreams to come true, God gave the Pharaoh two dreams that Joseph was able to interpret. This put Joseph smack into the middle of God's

plan and destiny for his life. *Genesis 41:14-16 & 39-40*   *14 So Pharaoh sent for Joseph, and he was quickly brought from the dungeon. When he had shaved and changed his clothes, he came before Pharaoh. 15 Pharaoh said to Joseph, "I had a dream, and no one can interpret it. But I have heard it said of you that when you hear a dream you can interpret it." 16 "I cannot do it,"*
Joseph replied to Pharaoh, "but God will give Pharaoh the answer he desires."
9 Then Pharaoh said to Joseph, "Since God has made all this known to you, there is no one so discerning and wise as you. 40 You shall be in charge of my palace, and all my people are to submit to your orders. Only with respect to the throne will I be greater than you."

PRAYER: Father, restore my dreams today and heal my past disappointments so I can become everything You have created me to be. Let me dream big again. Holy Spirit, awaken the dream in me. Help me to fulfill that dream!

ACTIVATION: Write down any unfulfilled or stagnant dreams. Ask God to revive them and you! Note what God does to accomplish this.

15

Where's Your Pain Relief?

Daily, I am becoming more aware of how many people in this world are walking around in pain. Physical pain, emotional pain, and spiritual pain caused by a variety of circumstances. This world is full of pain. Jesus Christ came so that we could live pain free. Why are so many of us living with so much pain? Many people do not know that they can live without pain. Many have no resources to alleviate the pain or get help. There are many reasons. God is revealing to us that know Him how to become the light and pain relievers in a world of so much pain. We must be aware of where we need healing first, allow the Lord to heal us, then bring the good news of that healing to others. Many times we have to let go of past hurts and disappointments to alleviate the emotional and sometimes physical pain. We have to get out of our past trauma and move forward into our future. Pain can be defined as a symptom of some physical hurt or disorder; emotional

distress; a fundamental feeling that people try to avoid such as the pain of loneliness. It can be a somatic sensation of acute discomfort. Trouble can cause bodily suffering to make sick or indisposed, cause emotional anguish or make miserable such as "it pains me to see my children not being taught well in school." It can be an annoyance, a cause of trouble, a source of unhappiness. Pain indicates that something is not right and needs attention. We want to help alleviate the discomfort. I took a first aide course

where we learned procedures for traumatic injuries. Many procedures would not be what our instincts tell us are correct. We would naturally want to pull something impaled into an arm out, thinking that would help, when it could cause more harm than good. The Lord is teaching us to ask Him how to help. Fixing things for others our way may not be God's best way to bring someone to wholeness. He has a plan for healing, but we must ask Him what our part is and how He wants to heal. We must always point others to the Healer, the Comforter who has the answer. He is the healer of the broken and the broken hearted.

Luke 4:18-19 "*The Spirit of the Lord is on me, because he has anointed me to proclaim good news to the poor. He has sent me to proclaim freedom for the prisoners and recovery of sight for the blind,to set the oppressed free, [19] to proclaim the year of the Lord's favor.*"

PRAYER: Jehovah Raphe, You are the Lord My Healer. Manifest yourself in my life today. Bring healing to my body, soul and spirit. Equip me to pray for others in pain. In Jesus name, Amen.

ACTIVATION: Ask the Lord to show you any place that you need healing. Ask Him to heal you and then to show you someone else in pain that He wants to heal and pray for them.

16

Get Your House in Order

It is time for deliverance out of our past bondages! I was unaware of the total meaning of 'Seder' and the Passover season until the past few years. One Spring I felt driven to clean and get my house in order. You know, that deep cleaning stuff that we tend to put off. It started when my dog got sick and of course there had to be some cleaning up. That sparked a strong desire to 'clean out' closets, drawers and

cabinets, that had been ignored for most of the winter. Surprisingly, it was as if I could see the disorder that I had been blinded to. I could not seem to stop. I opened drawers and realized I had not cleaned out old stuff in at least six months. Now it bothered me. I felt like I was nesting for the birthing of a new thing. Some may not know what the nesting instinct is. This is basically the uncontrollable urge to clean your house and generally go crazy doing all sorts of cleansing, and organizing, for the new member of a family. This is a primal instinct; all the females of almost

every species in the world will go through it in one way or another. I

realized that the Lord was ordering my steps into the next season. It was time to clean out and throw away what was not needed from the past season and get things in order to make room for what God was bringing in the new season. God desires for us to be acutely aware of how we may have allowed leaven (or sin) in our spiritual houses so that we do not allow it in the next season. This is what happens before the Seder dinner for Passover. They remove all the leaven from the

house to get it ready for the new. When God puts His finger on an area that He wants us to look at to bring into order, we should be quick to change. The Holy Spirit is here to help us remove the old things that are hindering us and make room for the new things that God desires to give us. Before the Israelites passed over on the journey into their new lives, God led them to clean out and make a clean break from the old. He desires us to do the same thing.

Luke 12 says:

*Meanwhile, when a crowd of many
thousands had gathered, so that they
were trampling on one another, Jesus
began to speak first to his disciples,
saying: "Be on your guard against the
yeast of the Pharisees, which is
hypocrisy. There is nothing concealed
that will not be disclosed, or hidden that
will not be made known. What you have
said in the dark will be heard in the
daylight, and what you have whispered
in the ear in the inner rooms will be
proclaimed from the roofs."*

PRAYER: Search me, O God, and know
my heart; try me, and know my
thoughts; And see if there is any
wicked way in me, please lead me in the
way everlasting. Shine Your light on

what needs to be discarded and what needs to be put in order. Amen

ACTIVATION: Ask the Lord to show you an area that He wants to reorder in your life. Then ask Him how to start and do what He tells you.

17

Increase Your Faith

I learned fear as a child and it was an integral part of me for much of my life. Many times God has led me to do things "afraid" to overcome certain fears. God has given us life in Christ and His Holy Spirit. If we are not double minded, we have faith and will believe God, and His Word. If what we believe is His Word and not just our good ideas, He watches over His Word to perform it. In June 2011 there was a tornado in our city.

During that tornado the Lord reminded me of an experience with my daughter when she was young. We were attending a family reunion for my husband's family at his uncle's cabin.

Patty L. Graham

We were fishing in the pond, just having
fun, when a huge storm blew up. The
sky grew dark and the wind began
blowing extremely hard. We all ran into
the small cabin and began watching the
news to see what was happening. You
could hear the storm roaring outside
and feel the tension inside. My
daughter, who was about six years old
at the time, climbed into my lap and fell
asleep. I held her, prayed and knew
everything would be fine. Jesus
fell asleep in the middle of a storm on
the lake in a boat with His disciples. He
told them to get in the boat and go to
the other side of the lake. They only
knew what they perceived and were
experiencing was a bad storm. Soon,
they discovered that God was in the

boat with them and they had nothing to fear.

Mark 4:35-40 says:

That day when evening came, he said to his disciples, "Let us go over to the other side." Leaving the crowd behind, they took him along, just as he was, in the boat. There were also other boats with him. A furious squall came up, and the waves broke over the boat, so that it was nearly swamped. Jesus was in the stern, sleeping on a cushion. The disciples woke him and said to him, "Teacher, don't you care if we drown?" He got up, rebuked the wind and said to the waves, "Quiet! Be still!" Then the wind died down and it was completely calm.

He said to his disciples, "Why are you

so afraid? Do you still have no faith?"

Jesus addressed the disciples' faith after this display of His authority. The disciples had been with Him and seen miracles, but at this point

shifted into fear instead of faith. Many of us do the same thing. In the midst of crisis, instead of faith kicking in, we look at everything around us and shift into fear. Our faith is powerful when we put it in the Lord. When we take our eyes off of Him and focus on our circumstances we sometimes lose our faith perspective. Today ask God to increase your faith. Then climb up into His lap and rest in His presence.

PRAYER: Lord, show me where I am not believing You and operating in fear instead of faith. Help me today to get

my eyes back onto You and see what
You are doing. In Jesus name, AMEN.

ACTIVATION: Ask the Lord to show you
any area of fear that you may have.
Ask Him how to face that fear and begin
to move in that direction in faith. Note
how God meets you when you move out
of fear into faith.

Patty L. Graham

18

Let's Be the Answer

I watched a television program one day
that really moved me to change the way
I operate. They did an experiment to
see how many people would respond to
an emergency situation in a public
place. Two ladies were sent into a busy
food court at a local shopping mall. One
lady pretended to faint while the other
scrambled around looking for people to
help. They repeated this three different
times. Interestingly, the only people
that ever helped the ladies were those
who were medically trained. Other
people mostly sat and continued to eat
and just stare at the ladies. When they
asked the other people afterwards what

they were thinking while they watched the two ladies, most of the people said they were looking to see if anyone was qualified to help. They expected someone else to help the ladies. The program then showed a short training about what to do to help someone who faints. The Lord revealed to me that this is what much of His church has been doing. We are eating our spiritual food to prepare to minister to a hurt world, but the world is hurting and we are not responding. It is time to respond!

Luke 10:30-36 gives us a story that illustrates this:

In reply Jesus said: "A man was going down from Jerusalem to Jericho, when he was attacked by robbers. They

*stripped him of his clothes, beat him
and went away, leaving him half dead.
A priest happened to be going down the
same road, and when he saw the man,
he passed by on the other side. So too,*

*a Levite, when he came to the place and
saw him, passed by on the other side.
But a Samaritan, as he travelled, came
where the man was; and when he saw
him, he took pity on him. He went to
him and bandaged his wounds, pouring
on oil and wine. Then he put the man
on his own donkey, brought him to an
inn and took care of him. The next day
he took out two denarii and gave them
to the innkeeper. 'Look after him,' he
said, 'and when I return, I will
reimburse you for any extra expense
you may have.'*

"Which of these three do you think was a neighbor to the man who fell into the hands of robbers?"

We do not have to wait for a disaster or crisis to help hurting people. There are plenty of people who need to know the love of God. Let's be the answer for those who are hurting today. Take the challenge to be the one who shares the love of Christ to someone who is hurting. God will give you encounters if you ask.

PRAYER: Lord, increase my faith to be the one you send to see people's lives changed. Lead me to bless others and reveal Your love to a lost and hurting world. Amen.

ACTIVATION: Ask God to give you encounters with those around you or whose path you cross that will encourage, bless and bring needed help. Note how God causes encounters to occur. I promise He will!

19

Heavenly Provision Is Coming

We live in the country where we see
wildlife all the time. We see rabbits,
snakes, squirrels, deer, roadrunners, all
types of birds, owls, hawks, vultures,
pheasant and even wild turkey. This is
new to me, always being a city girl. I
was not used to seeing all this wildlife,
but I am growing to love it. God has
made so many varied, beautiful and
unique creatures. One season I had
been praying about provision for the
vision that God had given us. I did not
seem to be getting the next phase of
His strategy and I was pressing Him for
some kind of direction. I was at home
on the phone and had left my gate

open. I looked outside and to my surprise saw a wild turkey run through my gate! I heard the Spirit of God say "My provision will come into your gates!" I laughed and tried to take a picture, but you might be surprised at how fast a turkey can run when he thinks you are after him. The next day I told my husband about the turkey and he laughed and said, "I was sitting on

the back patio when a turkey was flying over and fell from the sky into our back yard!" I've never seen anything like that. Again, the Lord said "My heavenly provision for your vision is coming." Since then we have moved our ministry in with another ministry and God has caused a great increase in every area. God is faithful. When He gives us a vision to fulfill for the Kingdom of God,

He also provides all that we need. Many times we must seek Him for His strategy, but when we follow that strategy, He faithfully provides.

Psalm 144:12-13 Then our sons in their youth   will be like well-nurtured plants, and our daughters will be like pillars   carved to adorn a palace. Our barns will be filled with every kind of provision. Our sheep will increase by thousands by tens of thousands in our fields;

PRAYER: Lord, show me the strategies that You have to bring provision for your people. Reveal the vision You have for me and the provision to bring Your Kingdom to the earth. In Jesus name I pray, amen.

ACTIVATION: Ask the Lord for His NOW strategy for new levels of provision. Then ask Him what to do first.   Note what begins to happen.

20

What Sound Do You Respond To?

My cell phone is set with special individual ring tones for different people so that I know who is calling me. Close family members have a ring that represents who they are to me. My son's is a drum, my husband's is a guitar, my daughter's is a marimba. My friends have different ring tones as well. The sound tells me if it is someone that I need to answer immediately or if it is someone not as close to me who can wait. This is the same way with our words and prayers to God. God responds to our faith filled words and prayers with righteous. He also responds to our cry when we need Him.

Patty L. Graham

The more we pray and spend time with God, the more He responds. He may not answer our doubt, negative decrees, or fear based requests because they are not a sound that He works or creates with. We are the ones He chooses to create through. Our sounds must align with God's to bring about His will. We are creative beings, made in the image of God. We are the only beings on

earth that have the ability to create. God created us in His image and told us to multiply and prosper. His plan has not changed. The plan was interrupted with the distraction to sin in the garden. So God sent Jesus to restore us to the original plan, with even more abundance than before. To receive that, we must choose to agree with God rather than with the snake that deceived in the garden and got Eve to agree with him. The deceiver got a response from Eve that was contrary to what God had said. We must choose to not respond to or act on the sounds that are contrary to God's will and voice. That's the WRONG SOUND. We must train ourselves to reject the sounds that do not produce life and life abundantly. Then we must train ourselves to RESPOND AND ACT on God's Words.

Jesus said this in Matthew 12:34-36

You brood of vipers, how can you who are evil say anything good? For the mouth speaks what the heart is full of. A good man brings good things out of the good stored up in him, and an evil man brings evil things out of the evil stored up in him. But I tell you that

Patty L. Graham

everyone will have to give account on the day of judgment for every empty word they have spoken.

PRAYER: Lord, teach me how to hear your voice. Another voice I will not follow. Forgive me for idle words I have spoken. Forgive me for believing lies and being deceived. You promised I could hear and follow your voice. Help me to put Your Word in my heart so that I won't sin against You. Thank You for hearing my prayers and answering me. Amen.

ACTIVATION: Ask the Lord to show you any place that you have believed and agreed with a lie. Repent and receive forgiveness. Ask Him to show You His

Word that replaces the lie and act on it.
Note how the change effects you and
those around you.

21

Keep Your Connections Strong

Change can be difficult. God is a God that changes not, yet He is continually taking us through changes to transform us into His image. Sometimes we don't understand or like the changes, but if we can hear the voice of the Lord even in the dark times, He will lead us. Psalms 23 illustrates this. My son went to college in Florida for a while. We communicated via phone and computer. One day a tropical storm system blew through Orlando and lightning hit his building, effectively frying his computer. This form of communication was now out. Within a few hours, his cell phone went black and he couldn't read texts or get his telephone numbers or see who was calling. He could call his father and I because he had our numbers memorized. We suggested he get a Go phone so he could communicate to get his computer fixed and tell the university what had happened, because much of his work was via computer. This all required extra work. He had to do things differently than planned, but was able to accomplish what he needed to. God will always help us find a way to get where He wants us. We must stay connected to God, listen to His voice, know His Word, and follow His instructions. He tells us to stay connected to Him and His body so we are not alone. Sometimes we may have to do things differently, and it may be uncomfortable, but God will help us if we ask Him.

Psalms 23 says this: The Lord is my shepherd, I lack nothing. He makes me lie down in green pastures, he leads me beside quiet waters, he refreshes my soul. He guides me along the right paths for his name's sake. Even though I walk through the darkest valley, I will fear no evil, for you are with me; your rod and your staff, they comfort me.

PRAYER: Lord, help me to comprehend the changes You want to make in my life and make me willing to do it Your way. Today, help me to connect with You in a deeper relationship and to walk with You through changes. Amen

ACTIVATION: Ask the Lord to remind you of a time of change that was hard but produced something new in you.

Ask Him to show You how He wants to work in your life to bring change today. Note what He says.

22

I Hope You _____

I have danced and taught dance for much of my life. It brings me much joy to express myself and what God is saying through movement, as well as teaching others to do the same. I enjoy dancing in worship as well as for fun. God gave me this gift and it causes life in me and in the atmosphere around me when I do what I was created to do. The Bible says in Colossians 3:23

Whatever you do, work at it with all your heart, as working for the Lord, not for human masters,

There have been wilderness seasons where I felt that God had me lay that gift down for one reason or another.

When something doesn't bring you joy anymore you need to ask God what is happening. So I did just that for a season. One day I was driving and had a vivid vision. It always amazes me how we can do both of those things at the same time – BUT GOD is able to help us do just that. I saw praise to God in the highest form, with colors, dance, lights, and heaven opening and joining us. Wow. I asked God what He wanted me to understand and do with this revelation. He clearly answered me saying "I want you to do what you see!" My spirit leapt, although I was not quite sure if my body would still do that. I called a friend who confirmed this and then I began doing what the Lord told me to do to accomplish His will. Within a week, I received dance shoes of almost every kind. I received, ballet, jazz, and ballroom dance shoes! Now that was a confirmation. The Lord showed me that I was to move in faith in a new way. He brought the following song by Lee Ann Womack to mind. As you read the words of the song, ask Holy Spirit what He would have you do in faith this year. Then insert that word where it says "Dance".

I hope you never lose your sense of wonder
You get your fill to eat but always keep that hunger
May you never take one single breath for granted
God forbid love ever leave you empty handed

Patty's Parables

I hope you still feel small when you
stand beside the ocean
Whenever one door closes I hope one
more opens
Promise me that you'll give faith a
fighting chance
And when you get the choice to sit it out
or dance
I hope you dance, I hope you dance
I hope you never fear those mountains
in the distance
Never settle for the path of least
resistance
Living might mean taking chances but
they're worth taking
Lovin' might be a mistake but it's worth
making
Don't let some hell bent heart leave you
bitter

When you come close to selling out

reconsider

Give the heavens above more than just

a passing glance

And when you get the choice to sit it out

or dance

I hope you dance (time is a wheel in

constant motion always)

I hope you dance (rolling us along)

I hope you dance (Tell me who wants to

look back on their years and wonder)

I hope you dance (where those years

have gone)

I hope you still feel small when you

stand beside the ocean

Whenever one door closes I hope one

more opens

Promise me that you'll give faith a

fighting chance

And when you get the choice to sit it out

or dance

I hope you

_____

PRAYER: Father, increase my faith today to become what You created me to become. Holy Spirit, stir up my faith to respond to You so that I may believe I can do all things through Christ Jesus. Stir up the desire in me today, to fulfill what was in Your heart when You put me in the earth. Amen.

ACTIVATION: Ask God to show You what was on His heart when He created YOU. Write that down and ask Him to help you become what He created you to be. Ask Him what He would have you do today to begin to be that.

Patty L. Graham

23

What Are You Wearing?

One of my favorite television programs
was <u>What Not To Wear.</u> The premise of
the program was to help a person
revamp their wardrobe by teaching
them what looked good on them.
Friends and family members sent a
request to the program. They secretly
videoed the person for a week, then
they would do an intervention. They
went to the closet of the person who
would receive the makeover and asked
them to pick outfits to model that they
liked to wear. Then they would do a full
mirror exam and discuss why they
thought these garments were attractive
on themselves. The experts would then
work with the person to find out what

their style was and would help them
project the best look to reflect who they
really were. They helped them to
discard their whole wardrobe and gave
them guidelines to buy a new wardrobe
with a $5000 credit card. The experts
would try to help them select a new
wardrobe that projected who they really
wanted to be in the future. This was
sometimes very emotional. Many of us
have a hard time breaking out of our
past issues due to wrong mindsets and
perceptions about who we are. These
people received a whole makeover from
head to toe and then presented that to
their friends and family. This was a life
changing event as the individuals
discovered how they truly could project
who they were created to be. This
really did take a renewing of their

minds. We identify people by their
garments. We identify many people's
occupations by their garments, such as
policemen, firemen, nurses, doctors,
military, etc. We wear spiritual
garments as well a physical garments.
The spiritual realm sees you in these
spiritual garments. When we wear
something that doesn't align with who
God says we are, we attract that
spiritual atmosphere. So what are you
wearing? Does it project who you are
spiritually? Or is it something that the
enemy or a person has put on you?
Joseph wore a garment of favor,
Mordecai wore a garment of authority
and John wore a prophet's garment.
Romans 13:12-14 tells us,

*The night is nearly over; the day is
almost here. So let us put aside the*

deeds of darkness and put on the armor of light. Let us behave decently, as in the daytime, not in carousing and drunkenness, not in

sexual immorality and debauchery, not in dissension and jealousy. Rather, clothe yourselves with the Lord Jesus Christ, and do not think about how to gratify the desires of the flesh.

PRAYER: Father, forgive me for wearing garments that you didn't give me to wear such as guilt, heaviness, and shame. I desire to change the garments that are not from you, for your garments of favor and sonship. Lord help me to put on the garments of the identity that you have given me. Thank you for New garments! Amen.

Patty L. Graham

ACTIVATION: Ask the Lord to show you
any 'garments' that other's have put on
you or that you have taken that do not
reflect Jesus and the identity that He
has given you. Actively remove those
and replace them with the identity
Christ has given you. Note how this
changes your perception of who you
are.

24

Can You Hear Me Now

Many times we have disconnects or
faulty transmissions on our cell phones
and communications. This is irritating
to say the least. God loves us so much
that He sent Jesus to reconcile us back
to Him, so we could be connected to
Him all the time. He sent His Holy Spirit
so we could all hear Him clearly and
walk with Him in authority and power.
There are plenty of distractions and
irritations in this world, but God has
provided a way for us to stay tuned to
Him to walk through it.

John 16:13 says

But when he, the Spirit of truth, comes,
he will guide you into all the truth. He
will not speak on his own; he will speak

*only what he hears, and he will tell you
what is yet to come.*

God speaks to us via Holy Spirit. We
can hear Him and know what He is
saying to us today. He will even talk to
you when you don't want to hear from
Him, just like Saul who was persecuting
God's people. God decided it was time
to have a discussion with Saul about a
change of attitude.

Acts 9:3-7

*As he neared Damascus on his journey,
suddenly a light from heaven flashed
around him. He fell to the ground and
heard a voice say to him, "Saul, Saul,
why do you persecute me?" "Who are
you, Lord?" Saul asked.*

*"I am Jesus, whom you are
persecuting," he replied. "Now get up*

and go into the city, and you will be told what you must do." The men travelling with Saul stood there speechless; they heard the sound but did not see anyone.

As a matter of fact, everyone with Saul heard Jesus' voice!! This changed history. Saul became Paul and the church was changed.   I am blessed to work with a healing ministry team that hears and obeys God. I had been very busy and missed arranging a ministry team for some healing room appointments. On the way to the building I prayed and asked the Lord to speak to some of the team to come. When I walked in the building, three members of the team were there and my assistant had brought me a cappuccino! Double blessings!! They all received God's communications to be at the healing rooms that morning, not mine. It's such a blessing to know that we can all hear God's voice and that if we obey, He will make sure we are where He needs us to be, doing what He desires for us to do. So many of us make hearing God's voice way too complicated.

Jesus said in John 10:4-5

When he has brought out all his own, he goes on ahead of them, and his sheep follow him because they know his voice. But they will never follow a stranger; in fact, they will run away

from him because they do not recognize a stranger's voice."

PRAYER: Father, give me ears to hear what your Holy Spirit is saying to me today. Holy Spirit, help me to obey and see you move gloriously in my life. In Jesus name, Amen

ACTIVATION: Write down what you believe Holy Spirit is saying to you today. If He tells you to do something, obey and see what happens. Note how God moves in your life today.

25

Believe for the Impossible

What seems impossible to you? Have you ever seen God do something that totally changed your perception of what is possible with God? God's Word tell us that all things are possible with God, but most of us do not really believe that. My sister and I were in a parking lot after a church service when we encountered a lady we did not know who was having trouble starting her car. We asked a young man that we were acquainted with to look at the engine. He did and pointed out to us that a part was missing and the engine would not start because the part must have come off that would make the connection for

the engine to start. He told us it would
not start until the part was replaced.
The lady did not have any other options
at that point and really needed her car.
My sister and I decided to ask the Lord
to do something impossible. We laid
hands on the car and prayed. The lady
got in and the car started. Later, she
told us that she drove the car without
the part until she could afford to get it
fixed. And YES, the part was missing
and the
mechanics agreed that was impossible!!
This is impossible in the natural, but we
serve a supernatural God who does
supernatural things. He created us in
His image to be supernatural beings in
the earth who are not limited to natural
means. God decided to prove Himself in
this event. God greatly desires to reveal

Himself to us in our every day lives.
Matthew 19:25-27 (NIV)

When the disciples heard this, they were greatly astonished and asked, "Who then can be saved"

Jesus looked at them and said, "With man this is impossible, but with God all things are possible."

PRAYER: Lord, the disciples asked you to help them with their unbelief. Today, I ask that you would help me to believe your Word. You desire to show your mighty works every day in my life and in the lives of those around me. Jesus reveal yourself today! Help me to grow in faith! Amen

ACTIVATION: Ask the Lord to show you something to pray for that seems impossible to you. Ask Holy Spirit to help You pray God's perfect will into that situation to see His glory. Note what happens!

Patty L. Graham

26

Enjoy the Process

I had been experiencing some fatigue
and physical issues that could have
been related to low thyroid levels.
Years ago I had 90% of my thyroid
removed and have been taking
medication ever since. The issues I was
having were typical of when you do not
have enough thyroid hormones. My old
doctor that I had seen for years had
moved into a new place and it was
going to take weeks to get in to see her,
so I decided to try to get into a new
clinic closer to me. I didn't know any of
these doctors, so I prayed and told God
that if I didn't like this one I'd go to my
other doctor, but I wanted to get things

121

checked out now. I went to see him and so far so good. There were some issues with thyroid, but he ran other tests, changed my meds and asked me to come back in a week. When I went back he said my cholesterol was dangerously high, and yes, the number was bad. Heart disease runs in my family and my dad died of a heart attack so I knew this was an issue. The doctor then gave me two choices to change the issue. He said, " You can continue to eat like you have been, and take this medication. These are the side effects of this medicine." The list was awful! "OR you can change your diet and eat a plant based diet, meaning nothing from animals, no cheese, eggs, meat, butter, or milk." Ok, that sounded pretty awful too since those were the foods that I mostly ate. Everything had cheese and butter in it! I asked how long it would take to see results. He was happy to tell me that with the diet change I should see progress in two weeks. If I continued to eat like I had been and took the meds, it would take about three months. That made my decision much easier. So I chose to change my diet. This was not as easy as it would have been to just take a pill, but the list of side effects and the length of time didn't sound appealing either. The doctor said that I needed to get my cholesterol down now! So, I began the new diet. It was a big change for me, but pretty soon it became a journey that I am now enjoying. After the first two weeks I went back and there was a 20% change. Very dramatic. This has become a new discipline and a process that I am learning to enjoy. Instead of looking at what I cannot eat, I am looking at what I can eat and how to make foods that are enjoyable. I had never thought I would be doing this but God has given me clarity, creativity, and revelation about this process. Many times we want the easy path when God wants us to enjoy the process and learn from Him as we are changing. Our transformation into His image will take a lifetime so we might as well cooperate with the one who created us. Rather than complaining, like the Israelites complained in the wilderness, let's cooperate and see what God will do on the way. The Israelites could have entered the Promised Land in thirty days, but because of their attitude, it

took forty years. Oh my! I am grateful
that God made a way for me to get
healthy and stay healthy so that I can
enter His promises.

Psalm 100

Shout for joy to the Lord, all the

earth. Worship the Lord with

gladness; come before him with joyful

songs.

Know that the Lord is God.   It is he

who made us, and we are his; we are

his people, the sheep of his pasture.

PRAYER: Lord, thank you for showing
me the processes of change You have
for me. Today, help me to be thankful
for where you have me and reveal how

I can cooperate with you to get where you want me to go.

ACTIVATION: Ask the Lord to show you any changes that He would have you make to help you get to the place in life He desires. Note what He tells you and begin the process.

27

What Part Are You?

We really do need people as well as
God. There was an old song that said
"people who need people are the
luckiest people in the world." I don't
know about it being lucky but I do know
that it is God's intention for us to
connect with other people to become
the body of Christ. One time I was
blessed by some friends with a gift of a
therapeutic massage. I have had
massages before, but this one really
relieved a lot of pain. So much so, that
I left with the realization that I had been
walking around in a lot of pain that I
didn't realize I had. What really
impressed me was that this massage
therapist would work on one area of my

body, and a different area would pop or the pain would release. Immediately this scripture about unity and diversity in the body of Christ came to my mind: *1 Corinthians 12:12-26*

Just as a body, though one, has many parts, but all its many parts form one body, so it is with Christ. For we were all baptized by one Spirit so as to form one body—whether Jews or Gentiles, slave or free—and we were all given the one Spirit to drink. Even so the body is not made up of one part but of many. Now if the foot should say, "Because I am not a hand, I do not belong to the body," it would not for that reason stop being part of the body. And if the ear should say, "Because I am not an eye, I do not belong to the body," it would not for that reason stop being part of the body. If the whole body were an eye, where would the sense of hearing be? If the whole body were an ear, where would the sense of smell be? But in fact God has placed the parts in the body, every one of them, just as he wanted them to be. If they were all one part, where would the body be? As it is, there are many parts, but one body. The eye cannot say to the hand, "I don't need you!" And the head cannot say to the feet, "I don't need you!" On the contrary, those parts of the body that seem to be weaker are indispensable, and the parts that we think are less honorable we treat with special honor. And the parts that are unpresentable are treated with special modesty, while our presentable parts need no special treatment. But God has put the body together, giving greater honor to the parts that lacked it, so that there should be no division in the body, but that its parts should have equal concern for each other. If one part suffers, every part suffers with it; if one part is honored, every part rejoices with it.

That always reminds me of the song we would sing as kids about how the knee bone's connected to the thigh bone and how all the bones are connected to make up our body. We really do need each other. If we understood how the body of Christ worked, we would quit trying to be the wrong part. We might even respond to each other the way the Bible says to. How we respond to the other parts of the body is so important

that our lives could depend on it. We
must be who God created us to be and
respect and love one another to become
whole and fulfil God's will in the earth.

PRAYER: Lord, reveal any source of
pain in my life that You want to deal
with. Show me where I may have
caused pain in others. Please bring
healing to me and to those around me
who need your healing touch. I agree
with Jabez's prayer: "and Jabez called
on the God of Israel saying, Oh that you
would bless me indeed, and enlarge my
territory, that your hand would be with
me, and that You would keep me from
evil, that I may not cause pain! So God
granted him what he requested."

ACTIVATION: Ask the Lord to show you
anyone that you need to pray for that
may be hurting. Call or send a note to
that person telling them you are
praying. Note what happens.

28

Face Your Fear

Many times, in order to deal with fears we must face what we fear. Fear and grief can paralyze us. I used to really fear public speaking. It is one of the number one fears of most adults. I could teach and speak to children all day long, but would get very anxious about speaking to adults. The thought of it would make my heart race, I would shake, and speak very fast. The Lord finally said, "Just look at them as though they are all children, because they are my children. Assume they have never heard anything like what I have given you to share and watch the change." When I did this, an anointing came and the presence of the Lord would be so strong that revelation flowed in a new way. So, this is the way I try to approach every speaking or teaching time. I trust that the Lord will speak through me and that His children will hear what He is saying, not me. That removes a lot of pressure. There are numerous stories in the Bible about 'facing fear' and seeing God show up. 2 Kings 7 talks about a time of great famine and fear in Israel. They were surrounded by their enemies. Doom and gloom filled their atmosphere. Elisha prophesied to the King that within 24 hours there would be a total change in their economy. Four lepers outside the city began to discuss their future and how they might change some things by facing a few fears.

2 Kings 7:3-16

Patty L. Graham

*Now there were four men with leprosy
at the entrance of the city gate. They
said to each other, "Why stay here until
we die? If we say, 'We'll go into the*

*city'—the famine is there, and we will
die. And if we stay here, we will die. So
let's go over to the camp of the
Arameans and surrender. If they spare
us, we live; if they kill us, then we die."*

*At dusk they got up and went to the
camp of the Arameans. When they
reached the edge of the camp, no one
was there, for the Lord had caused the
Arameans to hear the sound of chariots
and horses and a great army, so that
they said to one another, "Look, the
king of Israel has hired the Hittite and
Egyptian kings to attack us!" So they
got up and fled in the dusk and*

abandoned their tents and their horses and donkeys. They left the camp as it was and ran for their

lives. The men who had leprosy reached the edge of the camp, entered one of the tents and ate and drank. Then they took silver, gold and clothes, and went off and hid them. They returned and entered another tent and took some things from it and hid them also. Then they said to each other, "What we're doing is not right. This is a day of good news and we are keeping it to ourselves. If we wait until daylight, punishment will overtake us. Let's go at once and report this to the royal palace."

So they went and called out to the city gatekeepers and told them, "We went

*into the Aramean camp and no one was
there—not a sound of anyone—only
tethered horses and donkeys, and the
tents left just as they were." The
gatekeepers shouted the news, and it
was reported within the palace. The
king got up in the night and said to his
officers, "I will tell you what the
Arameans have done to us. They know
we are starving; so they have left the
camp to hide in the countryside,
thinking, 'They will surely come out, and
then we will take them alive and get
into the city.'" One of his officers
answered, "Have some men take five of
the horses that are left in the city. Their
plight will be like that of all the Israelites
left here—yes, they will only be like all
these Israelites who are doomed. So let
us send them to find out what*

happened." So they selected two chariots with their horses, and the king sent them after the Aramean army. He commanded the drivers, "Go and find out what has happened." They followed them as far as the Jordan, and they found the whole road strewn with the clothing and equipment the Arameans had thrown away in their headlong flight. So the messengers returned and reported to the king. Then the people went out and plundered the camp of the Arameans. So a seah of the finest flour sold for a shekel, and two seahs of barley sold for a shekel, as the Lord had said.

Today, be like the lepers. Step out of the fears and grief that are holding you back. Choose to take a step of faith.

Let the sound of heaven drive out those things that have stolen life and joy from you and change your life.

PRAYER: Father, today I give you my grief and fears. I choose to move out in faith where you lead and receive healing in my life for my future. In Jesus name, amen.

ACTIVATION: Ask the Lord to show you how to face a fear today. Obey what He tells you and note how you change.

29

Do You Have Hidden Pain?

When I was around 9 or 10 years old I loved sewing and making things that I would put on my dolls. The Summer of that year we were getting ready to go on vacation to see my aunt. I had been sewing and was running around my room putting things up and getting things ready to pack. I suddenly felt a sharp pain in my foot that ran up my leg and then felt something break off into my foot as I stepped all the way down on it. I looked on the floor and found half of a needle. I limped crying to my parents. They looked at my foot but could not see where the needle had gone into it. I had the other half in my hand, but because no one could see it

they weren't believing me. The pain
was intense. I showed my parents the
spot, but again there was no evidence
on the outside of my foot to prove that
the other half was in my foot. So, we
finished packing and left for the longest
three week vacation I had ever
experienced. I kept complaining and I
was having a hard time walking. My
Dad tried to find the needle by cutting
into my foot. This did not help, it just
made it worse and he could not find it.
It was too deep. I tried to have fun,
tried to skate, I was in too much pain.
Three or so weeks later, at home my
parents got me in to see a doctor. The
doctor X rayed the foot to see the
needle had calcified into the bone in my
foot. Finally, he removed the needle
and it began to heal. This is such a

picture of how many people are walking around with hidden wounds. From the outside, many times we cannot see the deep pain that is hindering their walk. Many times we don't even know the source of the pain, we just know the symptoms. God is the great physician, and is well able to look into our beings and reveal by Holy Spirit x-ray where the source of the pain is coming from and how to remove it. Once we take it to Him, the healing process can truly begin.

Jesus said: *Mark 2:17*

*On hearing this, Jesus said to them, "It is not the healthy who **need a doctor**, but the **sick**. I have not come to call the righteous, but sinners."*

PRAYER: Father, shine a light in me and reveal any hidden pain that is hindering my walk with you. Help me to remove that hindrance and begin my healing process. Use me to help those around me by taking them to THE GREAT PHYSICIAN to reveal their hidden pain and heal them as well. Thank You, Lord. Amen.

ACTIVATION: Ask God to lead you in removing all hindrances to your wholeness. Forgive as He leads and remove what He leads you to remove. Note how your healing process feels and sets you free.

30

What Is God Confirming

I teach a Spiritual Life class every week
to help people understand their
individual giftings and callings and how
to function in those giftings and callings.
This involves lots of scripture and
revelation. Weekly we share how and
what God has been revealing to us and
encourage one another. One week I
was in a bit of a battle and needed
prayer on the way to a meeting. I
called a friend who prayed for me over
the phone. One of the things she
prayed was that God would give me five
smooth stones to defeat the giants I
was facing, just as David had taken five
smooth stones to defeat Goliath. This
really stuck with me. I knew God was

speaking to me about facing some giants and that He had given me the weapons that I needed to win these battles. I went to one meeting and we agreed to arrange for more meetings with other people that needed to be there. These were confrontational meetings, but God was arranging them, and was clearly wanting me there. I agreed to obey God but asked Him to continue to help me through this battle. I then went to prepare for my class that evening. We had a great class. It was warm outside and still light so many of us went outside after class to visit and enjoy the evening. One young man had texted me to let me know that he was working late and was trying to get to class, but wasn't sure he would make it. I just assumed he would not get there that evening. As I began walking to my car to leave he sped into the parking lot. He looked as though he was on a mission. He jumped out of his car saying " Is class over? I was afraid I was going to miss you." I told him yes, class was over, and asked what was happening. He ran to his car and came back and asked me to open my hands. I did so and he dropped five smooth stones into my hand and said "God told me to get these to you tonight to win your battles." I almost cried. I confirmed to him that he had heard and obeyed God and that I would pray for God to bless him with more revelation like this. God wants to help us in every area of life, especially the hard times that we are battling through. He is faithful to confirm when we need to

know we are on the right track, even if
it is hard.

1 Corinthians 1:9
*God is **faithful**, who has called you into
fellowship with his Son, Jesus Christ our
Lord.*

PRAYER: Lord, thank you that you
know what I need to accomplish what
you give me to do. Today, encourage
me by confirming that I am on the right
track. Amen.

ACTIVATION: Ask the Lord specifically
about an area of your life that you need
His confirmation about. Note how He
affirms you.

31

Obedience Is Better Than Sacrifice

A few years ago the Lord led our
ministry group to begin crisis response
training. We have tornadoes and fires
in Oklahoma and we felt the Lord
leading us to get trained before the next
tornado season. We began training and
within three months there was a bad
tornado and many of us were blessed to
get to help in various ways. Until this
time, I had never experienced an
earthquake. There had been some in
our state, but not in our area. The Holy
Spirit kept urging me to remove a
picture that was above my bed because
when the earthquake came the picture
would fall on my head. I really felt that
this was the Lord, but we had never had

148

earthquakes. So, in obedience I removed the picture. A few months went by and there was no earthquake so I put the picture back because I really liked it there. The Lord would then impress me again to remove the picture with the same thought that it would hit me on the head when the earthquake happened. So, I removed it again. I waited. No earthquake, so I put it back. We are interesting creatures! One night about midnight I awoke to my bed shaking and my house quaking. I sat straight up in bed and said, "Forgive me Lord, I'm removing the picture right now!" Interestingly, I was not afraid of the earthquake, I was more concerned about disobeying God. At this point I realized that God will warn us, help us, teach us and guide us

through anything that we may face IF
we will obey Him knowing that He has
our best interest at heart. Since that
time we have had many earthquakes
and we have continued to train and to
help people in crisis. I have learned
that God is truly faithful. We just need
to obey His voice!

Psalms 25:4-5 says:

*Show me your ways, Lord, teach me
your paths.*

*Guide me in your truth and teach
me, for you are God my Savior,   and
my hope is in you all day long.*

PRAYER: Lord, make me more sensitive
to the promptings of Your Holy Spirit
today and help me to obey even when I
don't understand all the reasons or see

it in the natural. Thank you for helping me be obedient. Amen.

ACTIVATION: Ask the Lord to show you if there is something new He would have you do to prepare you for the future. Note what He says and how you obeyed.

Patty's Parables

End Notes

Chapter 2 *The Lord of the rings* [Motion picture].
  (2002). New Line Home Entertainment.
   pg. 7
   Tolkien, J. (1966). *The lord of the rings.*
   New York: Houghton Mifflin. pg. 7

Chapter 2   Dickson, John ℗ 2013 **The Swords Will Contend** Slingshot Media Group Released on: 2010-01-25 Auto-generated by YouTube. pg. 10

Chapter 3 Hine, Stuart K. 1953 *How Great Thou*
   Art. pg. 13

Chapter 4 Baum, L. Frank, August 15, 1939 **The Wonderful Wizard of Oz**. pg. 21

Chapter 9 Henry, M. (1997). *Matthew Henry's concise commentary on the whole Bible.* Nashville: T. Nelson. pg. 55

Patty L. Graham

Chapter 12 Oedekerk, Steve. June 22, 2007 *Evan Almighty,* Universal Pictures pg. 75

Chapter 22 Sanders, Mark D., Sillers, Tia 1999; *I Hope You Dance* Recorded by Lee Ann Womack March 2000 MCA Nashville, Produced by Mark Wright. pg. 133, 134

Chapter 23 [Television series episode]. *What Not to Wear.* TLC United States, BBC Worldwide Productions 2003-2013. pg. 138

Made in the USA
Coppell, TX
26 July 2021